W9-BNF-648

SIMPLE SCIENCE SAYS:
Take One Mirror

by Melvin Berger

illustrated by
G. Brian Karas

SCHOLASTIC INC.

New York Toronto London Auckland Sydney

No part of this publication may be reproduced
in whole or in part, or stored in a retrieval
system, or transmitted in any form or by any
means, electronic, mechanical, photocopying,
recording, or otherwise, without written
permission of the publisher. For information
regarding permission, write to Scholastic Inc.,
730 Broadway, New York, NY 10003.

ISBN 0-590-41613-8

Copyright © 1989 by Melvin Berger.
Illustrations © 1989 by Scholastic Books, Inc.
All rights reserved. Published by Scholastic Inc.

12 11 10 9 8 7 6 5 4 3 2 1   9/8 0 1 2 3 4/9

Printed in the U.S.A.   11

First Scholastic printing, January 1989

Contents

Can you see behind your back?
Can you look around corners?
Can you read backward writing?
Can you makc a rainbow?

Yes, you can!
All you need is a mirror.

**SIMPLE SCIENCE SAYS: Take the mirror
from the back of this book...
and discover how science can help you do
some amazing things.**

SIMPLE SCIENCE SAYS:
Look at yourself

Does your hair look neat?
Is your nose shiny?
Are there crumbs on your chin?
Do your eyes crinkle when you smile?

How can you find out?
Look at yourself in a mirror, of course!

Everyone knows what a mirror is.
But not everyone knows how a mirror
lets you see yourself.
Here's how a mirror works.

The light in the room shines on your face.
The light bounces off your face
and strikes the mirror.
The mirror sends back, or reflects, the light
to your eyes.
And you see your face in the mirror!

Most mirrors are made of glass.
On the back of the glass
is a thin layer of silver.
The glass and silver reflect the light rays
and you see the image.

But the mirror in this book is different.
It is made of a special shiny plastic.
The plastic mirror reflects light just
like a glass and silver mirror.

Prop your mirror up on a table.
Look at your reflection.
Now touch your right ear with your right hand.
Take a close look.
Which ear do you *seem* to be touching?
Why, it looks like it's your *left* ear!

What's going on?
What is your right ear doing
on your left side?

Mirrors reverse, or turn images around.
In a mirror, your right ear appears
on your left side.
If you lift your right hand,
your mirror image has its left hand in the air.
Blink your right eye and
it looks as if your left eye is closed.

Now try this:
Take your small mirror to a wall mirror.
Hold one edge of the small mirror against
the wall mirror with your left hand.

Touch your right ear with your right hand again.
Look at your image in the small mirror.
You may have to move your head
or tilt the small mirror.
But this time you'll see yourself
touching your *right* ear.
You'll see yourself as others see you.

The wall mirror picks up your image
and reverses it.
It reflects your image to the other mirror.
The small mirror reverses it again.

SIMPLE SCIENCE SAYS:
Push, bend, and twist

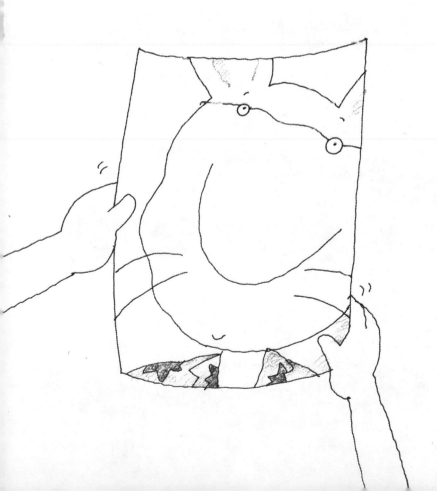

Many amusement parks have fun-house mirrors.
These mirrors change the way you look.
One mirror makes you look
as skinny as a telephone pole.
Another makes you look as fat as Santa Claus.

Fun-house mirrors do this
because they are not flat.
Some curve in.
Some curve out.
Some bend this way.
Some bend that way.

Hold the sides of your small plastic mirror
with two hands.
Slowly push your hands together.
Make the mirror bend *away* from you.

What happens to the image of your face?
At first it grows wider.
Keep bending the mirror.
Soon your image will grow another nose!

Hold the mirror flat once more.
Then slowly push both sides together.
But this time make the mirror bend *toward* you.
What happens to the image of your face?

Try bending the mirror in other ways.
Push on one corner.
Pull on another.
Twist it this way.
Twist it that way.
Make as many funny faces as you can.

SIMPLE SCIENCE SAYS:
Make a shadow box

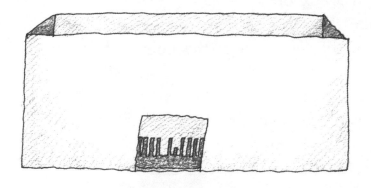

Light rays always move in straight lines—
always, that is, unless something
turns or bends them.
You can test this out.
All you need is an empty shoe box,
a comb, some tape, and a small flashlight.

First ask an adult to help you
cut a hole in the shoe box.
Cut the hole at the bottom
and near the center of a side panel.
Make it about 2 inches high and 2 inches wide.
Place the comb with the teeth up
inside the box and across the hole.
Tape the comb in place.

Set the box on a table.
Make the room as dark as possible.
Shine the flashlight at the hole and the comb.

Look inside the box.
Do you see shadows of the comb's teeth?
If you don't, move the flashlight
forward or back until you do.
Notice that the shadows go straight across the box.
Light rays move in straight lines.

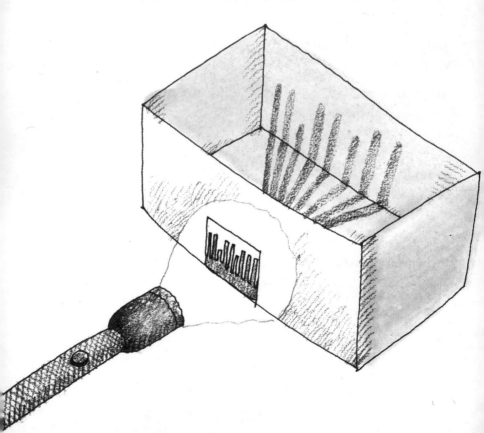

Now hold the mirror inside the box.
Hold it to catch the light from the flashlight.
Turn the mirror at an angle.
Watch the lines change direction
as they bounce off the mirror.
The mirror bends the light.
It sends the light rays off
along a different path.

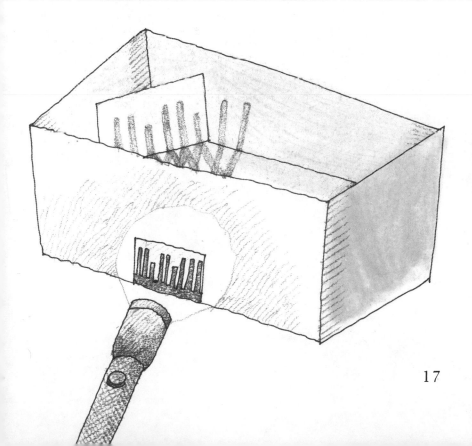

SIMPLE SCIENCE SAYS:
Make light bounce like a ball

Light bounces back
when it strikes a mirror.
It is like a ball
bouncing back
when it strikes
the floor.
And both light
and the ball
bounce back
in the same way.

Drop a ball straight down
and watch it bounce back.
Which way does it go?

The ball bounces
straight up.
Straight down.
Straight up.

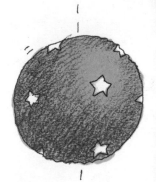

Now throw the ball to the floor
at a slight angle.
The ball does not bounce straight up.
It bounces up at a slight angle.
Slight angle down. Slight angle up.
Like a narrow letter

V

Try it again.
But this time throw the ball sideways
to the floor at a much bigger angle.
Notice how the ball bounces up
at a much bigger angle.
Big angle down. Big angle up.
Like a wide letter

V

Do you see what's happening?
The ball always bounces
at the same angle it is thrown.

A mirror reflects light
in the exact same way.
You can prove this.
In a dark room shine a small flashlight
at your mirror. Look at the light ray that goes
from the flashlight to the mirror.
Look at the light ray that is reflected
from the mirror to the wall.
Can you see that both light rays
are at the same angle?

Change the angle
by moving the flashlight this way and that.
Notice how the light always bounces off
the mirror at the same angle
it strikes the mirror.

SIMPLE SCIENCE SAYS:
Make a periscope

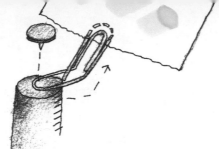

Find a long wooden pole or an old broom handle.
You'll also need a paper clip and a thumbtack.

Use the thumbtack to attach the paper clip
to one end of the pole.
Put the thumbtack through
the single-loop end
of the paper clip.

You may have
to use a hammer
if the wood
is very hard.
Ask a grown-up
to help you.

Next bend up the double-loop
end of the paper clip.
Hold the thumbtack down while you
bend the paper clip up.
Slip your mirror into the paper clip.

If you don't have a thumbtack,
you can use some strong tape instead.
First bend up the double-loop end
of the paper clip.
Then hold the single-loop against the end
of the pole, and tape the clip to the pole.

Now you can put your periscope to work for you.
See what's on a high shelf—
without getting on a ladder.
Check out who's on the other side of a doorway—
without leaving the room.
Know what's happening behind you—
without turning around.
See around a corner—
without going around the bend.

Your periscope works like this:
the mirror picks up light rays
from places you cannot see.
It changes the direction
of these light rays and
reflects them to your eyes.

SIMPLE SCIENCE SAYS:
Make a mirror flashlight

In a dark room, turn off all the lights but one.
It's best if this light is from a small bulb
in a table lamp, or a ceiling or wall fixture.

Stand near the light bulb.
Aim your mirror, half toward the light,
half toward a dark corner of the room.
See how the bright beam lights up
the dark corner?

Wiggle the mirror back and forth.
Watch the light swing back and forth, too.
The mirror catches the light
from the bulb and reflects it
around the room.
The reflected light is almost like
the light from a flashlight.

SIMPLE SCIENCE SAYS:
Crack a mystery code

Can you read this mystery-code letter?

Dear Max,
Meet me
at noon.
Jeff

Is this some strange new language?
These letters don't come from *our* alphabet.
Or do they?

Here's how to find out.
Hold the book up so
the mystery message faces your mirror.
Look into the mirror.

Mystery solved!
It's easy to read the message in the mirror.

You know that mirror images are in reverse.
So if something is written backwards,
it looks right in a mirror.

You can send a mystery message
to someone else.
The trick is to write
the letters and words backwards.
Print the letters and only use capitals.
And go from right to left.
Try it a few times.
You may have to practice before
you can do it well.
Each time you write a word,
check it with the mirror.
Make sure it looks right.

Use mirror writing to send
secret messages to a few friends.
All they need is a mirror
to discover the meaning.

SIMPLE SCIENCE SAYS:
Fool your eyes

Find another small mirror.
Also get a crayon, thick pen,
or marker that can stand by itself.

Prop one mirror on a table so that
it stands straight up and down.
Put the crayon a few inches
in front of that mirror.
Hold the other mirror in front
of the crayon.
Let the shiny side face the crayon.

Look at the propped-up mirror.
Do you see a whole row of crayons?
If not, wiggle the other mirror
back and forth until you do.

Can you guess why your eyes are fooled
and you see so many crayons
instead of just one?

Light bouncing off the crayon
is picked up by one mirror.
From there it is reflected
to the second mirror.
The second mirror reflects it back
to the first.
Then the first mirror reflects it back
to the second.
The image is reflected back
and forth from mirror to mirror,
and you see many images
of the same crayon.

SIMPLE SCIENCE SAYS:
Make a kaleidoscope

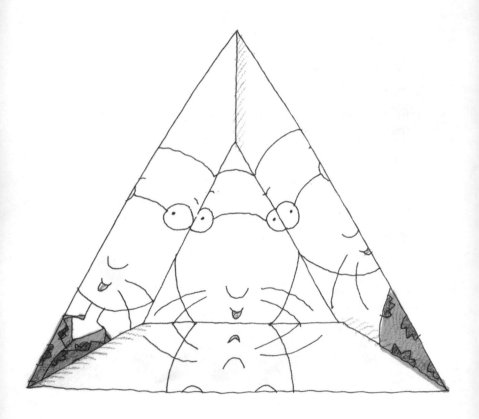

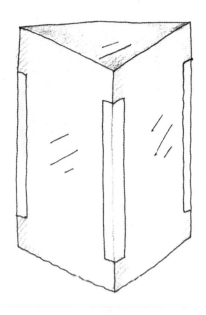

A kaleidoscope is a toy that makes
beautiful designs with mirrors.
You can make a simple kaleidoscope this way.

Trace and cut out two pieces of cardboard
the same size as your mirror.
Cover the cardboard carefully with
heavy aluminum foil about
one inch wider than the cardboard.
Be careful not to wrinkle or smudge
the aluminum foil.
Also, be sure to have the shiny side out.
Fold back the edges to hold the foil in place.
Now you have three mirrors.

Get a piece of blank, white, unlined paper.
Also collect several markers of different colors.
Cover the paper with a big colorful design.
Make—
—lines and curves
—squares and circles
—dots and dashes
—and any other shapes you can think of.

Hold the three mirrors so that
their long edges are touching.
Tape the mirrors together.
Your kaleidoscope is now ready to use.

Place the kaleidoscope over the design.
Look down into the center of the kaleidoscope.
Move it around the paper.
See how the colors and patterns keep changing.

The mirrors reflect the designs in different ways
as you move the kaleidoscope around.
What a show!

SIMPLE SCIENCE SAYS:
Try some letter magic

Does this look like any letter you know?

How about this?

Or this?

Here's another.

These scribbles don't look like any letters.
But you can change them into letters
with a little letter magic.

Hold your mirror straight up and down.
Place the edge exactly at the top
of each scribble.
What do you see?
There is an X, a D, an E, and a K!

All of these letters are the same in one way.
The top of each letter is the same
as the bottom—but in reverse.
Letters that are the same
on top and bottom are symmetrical.

From A to Z, our alphabet has
nine symmetrical capital letters.
Simple Science showed you four of them.
Can you guess the five others?

Here are the bottom halves.

DᑕᑎꓕU

Now do you know what they are?
Use your mirror to make sure.

SIMPLE SCIENCE SAYS:
Try some word magic

There are many words you can make
out of the nine symmetrical
letters—B, C, D, E, H, I, K, O, and X.

Here is one.

Hold your mirror along the top.
What is the word?

Here's another.

What word do you see in your mirror?

Are you ready to write words using
the symmetrical letters?
Write the bottom halves of the letters
on a piece of paper.
Then use your mirror to read them.

Try it first with DOCK and HIKE.
Then think up your own words or names
using the nine letters.

SIMPLE SCIENCE SAYS:
Do some mirror tricks

Get some pictures of friends or family members.
Be sure they are looking straight ahead.
Place the mirror along the line
of the person's nose.
Hold it so that you can see both
the photo and the image in the mirror.
Tilt the mirror to one side.
What does this do to the shape of the face?
Does it become wider or narrower?
Tilt the mirror the other way.
How does the face change this time?

Try the mirror at different angles.
You can even hold the mirror
across the face instead of up and down.
See how many silly faces you can create.

SIMPLE SCIENCE SAYS:
Make a rainbow

Wait for a bright, sunny day.
Get a baking pan with sides about
an inch or two high.
Fill it nearly to the top with water.
Place it on a table
where the sun will shine on it.

Set your mirror in the pan.
Lean it against the side where the sun strikes.
Put a small, flat dish in the pan
to keep the mirror from
slipping.

Now look around the room.
Find the spot on the wall or ceiling
where the sunlight is reflected.
Do you see a rainbow?

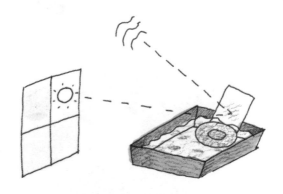

If you don't see a rainbow—
—be sure to wait until the water becomes still.
—slide the bottom of the mirror
forward or back in the pan.
—move the whole pan forward or back.
And you'll be sure to see a most beautiful rainbow.
Where does it come from?

Sunlight usually looks white.
But it is really made up of many colors.
Violet, indigo, blue, green, yellow, orange,
and red are all present in sunlight.

The water and the mirror
break the sunlight up into its separate colors.
The colors form a rainbow.
Sometimes it is hard to see each color separately.
The colors blend together.
But even if you cannot see them, they are all there.

SIMPLE SCIENCE SAYS:
Take one mirror—
and see what else you can
find out about mirrors
and what they do.